Behind•the•Scenes

T. R. Storey

Troll Associates

Jesse tossing Michelle over his shoulder.

Published by Troll Associates, Inc.

Printed in the United States of America.
10   9   8   7   6   5   4   3

Produced by Creative Media Applications, Inc.
Art direction by Fabia Wargin.

This book is dedicated to Andrew and Jessie.

Special thanks to Roy Wandelmaier, Sheryl Haft, Michelle Sucillon, Amy Weingartner, and Carole Franklin.

Table of Contents

Welcome to *Full House*!

Once upon a time . . .

A widowed young father named Danny Tanner decided he needed help raising his three daughters . . .

So he asked his brother-in-law, rock 'n' roller Jesse Katsopolis, and his best friend, Joey Gladstone, to move in and help him out.

The rest, as they say, is *Full House* history.

ABC's zany hit comedy is the first show to pack together 2 standup comics, 1 teen idol, 4 twins, 2 dogs, 2 teenage girls, 1 beautiful co-host, and endless laughs!

How would you like to go backstage and visit the stars? Do you want to go behind the scenes and see how the show is made? Then you've come to the right place.

Family looking at the first picture of the twins.

Happy Father's Day—
Meet Bob Saget

When Bob Saget was growing up, the only thing he wanted to be was a doctor. "I used to think that being a doctor was the only noble profession," says Bob.

Today, no one would turn to Saget to perform a big operation. Unless of course it's to have a funny bone tickled! As the star of two hit prime-time TV shows at once, the 36-year-old Saget has become one of the best-known, best-loved comics in the country.

D.J., Danny, Michelle, and Stephanie.

"It's wild, isn't it?" Bob asks, flashing a warm, winning grin. "*Full House* is my day job, *America's Funniest Home Videos* is my weekend job, and HBO is my night job. Wow, I worked for 12 years to get something going, and then within one month it all seemed to fall into place!"

A Comedian Is Born

Bob Saget was born on May 17, 1956, in Philadelphia. His father ran the meat department at a local super-market. In school, Bob confesses to having been a B-/C+ student. He scored his highest grades at cracking up his friends. "I knew I was funny when I was four," he remembers.

In high school, Bob started playing guitar and writing funny songs. "All bad," says Bob, who is known for being gentle with friends, but hard on himself.

He also began making up standup routines. Bob and his friends would practice them after school.

"One was about a gas that escaped," recalls Bob. "I go after it with a net, and I'm a hunchback. It was really stupid."

Getting parents to turn out for the experimental films proved to be a real chore. But it was a chore for which Bob had a special tool. With his humorous style, the tall teenager found he could always pack the house. He was already showing signs of being the perfect host.

In 1978, Bob was graduated from the film program

at Temple University in Philadelphia. He moved to Los Angeles, where he enrolled in the prestigious film program at the University of Southern California. Bob was intent on being a film director, but he lasted only three days. More school, he realized, just wasn't for him.

But what was?

Warming Up a Career

Bob's old high school friends all had the same suggestion. They remembered how he used to make them laugh. Why not bring those talents to a larger audience?

Bob soon found his way to the Comedy Store, Los Angeles' top comedy club. His gentle style proved to be perfect host material. In fact, Bob hosted at the club for the next ten years!

His reputation as a comic grew steadily as he started traveling around the country, playing local clubs. Bob describes his routine as "weird, kind of free-association. Sometimes the audience doesn't know what I'm talking about, and I don't know either!"

Bob's first television appearances included the comedy game show *Make Me Laugh* (clearly Bob was a natural for that assignment!), Rodney Dangerfield's *HBO Young Comedians Special,* and several commercials. But it was as a warm-up act that his career really began to—well—warm up.

Most TV situation comedies (sitcoms) are filmed in

front of live audiences. (Shows such as *Full House* are called situation comedies because each week they put their characters in different funny situations.) If the live audience at a TV show laughs a lot, it may encourage more laughter from the audience at home.

That's why on a sitcom, the producers—the bosses in charge of running the whole production—often hire a warm-up act. While the cast and crew make their final preparations, the warm-up comedian performs for the live audience. If the warm-up act is good enough, the live audience will provide plenty of hoots and howls when the show is taped.

Bob Saget was an expert at warming up crowds. In fact, he soon became a regular warm-up act for two young producers, Bob Boyett and Tom Miller, who have been responsible for some of TV's hottest shows. Audiences usually roar at Boyett-Miller shows, warm-up or no warm-up. Even so, the job Bob was doing greatly impressed his producers. They told themselves this young man was too talented to use simply as a

Michelle and Danny.

preview to the main event. Bob Saget appeared to be an event in himself!

Bob's career continued to grow. Miller and Boyett hired him for guest appearances on some of their shows. He performed briefly on comedies such as *Bosom Buddies* (which starred Tom Hanks), *It's A Living,* and *The Greatest American Hero,* and then he co-starred in the feature film *Critical Condition* with Richard Pryor.

But his really big break, Bob *thought,* came in 1987 when he landed a job as co-host on CBS's *The Morning Show.*

A Missing Chair

That big break soon fizzled. Six months into his new job, Bob arrived at work only to find his chair had been removed from the set. He was fired.

At least, says Saget, "the show's ratings dropped when I left. That made me feel good!"

As it turned out, though, Bob wasn't out of work for long. The busy producers Boyett and Miller were developing a new show. They needed someone to play the lead—a charming, funny widower named Danny Tanner. They picked Bob Saget, their old warm-up act. Bob was back on TV, and this time he was there to stay.

Bob and Dave's Excellent Reunion

Making the show even more of a dream job for Bob, the

Joey and Danny.

producers cast Bob's real-life best friend Dave Coulier as Danny Tanner's best friend! Bob and Dave had been pals for years. They had helped keep each other laughing through a hard decade, as they both struggled to make it in standup comedy.

"We're even closer in real life," says Bob. "We're like brothers." Laughing, he adds, "It's pretty weird—almost a cosmic joke—that we ended up on a sitcom together."

The show wasn't the only thing that was going wonderfully for Bob. Bob had married a woman named Sherri. They had known each other in high school, and began dating in college. The young couple soon began raising a Full House of their own. (They now have two daughters, Aubrey and Lara, and a third baby is on the way.)

By now, you'd think Bob would have been content. But Saget admits he doesn't experience contentment very often. On the show he plays a neat-freak; off-screen he admits to being a workaholic.

Bob's wish was granted. More work was on the way—and then some!

An Overnight Success

By now, *Full House* had become a nationwide hit. So when ABC needed a host for its new show, *America's Funniest Home Videos,* they called on a proven talent, Bob Saget. Suddenly Bob was hosting and co-writing a second show. And *Home Videos* was an overnight sensation.

As if that wasn't enough, Bob signed on to do a standup concert on HBO as well.

How does he manage? "I'm finding I can handle it," says Bob. He gives a great deal of the credit to his wife's support and understanding. But he's still not satisfied with himself.

Of course not. The grades he gives himself haven't improved much since the ones he got from his teachers in high school. For instance, he still feels he hasn't done anything that has really wowed audiences. "They might think I'm friendly and funny," he says. That's a major understatement.

Bob has relaxed about one thing, however. He no longer thinks being a doctor is the only worthwhile profession. After all, says Bob, "People need to laugh."

When TV viewers have that need, they know they can count on Bob Saget.

Behind the scenes at a backyard barbecue.

Thanks to D.J., Candace Cameron Has Two Families

Quick, who's your favorite teenage actress? If you're like many TV fans, you may have answered "Candace Cameron!"

Blond-haired and blue-eyed, Candace has been acting since she was five. She landed her most important role to date, D.J. (Donna Jo), at the mere age of ten. Now 16, Candace has already racked up a list of credits (including roles in TV and feature films) that would make any actor proud. On top of it all, she's never had a single acting lesson!

Why does performing come so naturally to her? Maybe it helps that she grew up with a star in the family!

D.J. and her cousin, played by Kirk Cameron.

Sibling Rivalry Among the Stars?

Born on April 6, 1976, in Los Angeles, Candace comes from a large, close-knit clan. She has two older sisters, Bridgette and Melissa, and an older brother you may have heard of—Kirk Cameron, star of *Growing Pains*!

That's a lot of celebrity for one household. But while Candace says she's close to her brother, she doesn't feel there's much sibling rivalry between them. He's always been there for her when she's needed him.

Of course, maybe it helps that the two don't discuss acting. "When we see each other, it's usually as family or to see what's going on," says Candace. "My brother and I have not really had a whole lot of discussion about acting or our careers."

Two Families

Candace has made many friendships on the *Full House* set. "Everyone on the set gets along really well. Bob

Saget and Dave Coulier are both equally funny but in their own ways. John Stamos is funny also. He's cool. We have a good time. But sometimes"—As if to prove her next point, Candace begins to giggle—"it gets to be too fun and we get off track."

Busy with show biz, Candace doesn't get to see as much of her own family as she would like. Luckily, her father on the show, Bob Saget, has been able to fill in the gaps.

"I like to hang out with him a lot because he's always cracking jokes. We're good friends. But whenever I have a problem, my real dad always stops and really listens. I think that's neat. Some parents can't always do that."

Growing Pains

There have been a lot of changes at the Cameron house lately. Kirk has moved to his own house in nearby Simi Valley. That meant Candace could stop sharing a room with her sister Bridgette and enjoy the luxury of a room of her own.

How did she decorate it? "I wanted it to be really plain and yet have a modern look. I didn't want it to be busy-looking because I wanted it to be a place where I could relax." So with her mom's help, Candace stripped the room's old wallpaper, painted the walls white, and brought in all black furniture.

Starring in a sitcom is hard work, and after a long

day on the set Candace needs to relax. Her favorite activities are hanging out with friends at their homes or the mall, and talking on the phone. She also likes going to the movies, especially if her favorite actors of all time—Jack Nicholson and Kevin Costner—are starring.

"I don't have a boyfriend or anything," says the attractive young actress, "and I'm not searching for one right now. I don't even have a crush on anyone. I know a lot of guys but I just like them as friends. I'm not really in a rush to date."

D. J. and Kimmy.

Would a Teenager Say That?

That's not true of D.J., the character she plays on TV. "D.J. is growing up and doing a lot of things I wouldn't do in my real life," admits Candace, "so I'm having a great time on the show!"

As D.J. tackles new problems, Candace often finds herself faced with new acting challenges. In one episode, the script called for her to break down and cry. "I didn't know if I'd be able to pull it off. But I was able to, and it was a great feeling! After I finished the scene, everyone was clapping!"

Part of the reason she enjoys her work so much, says Candace, is that the show's producers and directors are open to her input. They look to her for advice on "what a teenager would or wouldn't say," and occasionally she contributes to her character's story line.

Though she's only 16, Candace has already spent years in front of cameras. And she admits it's hard for her to imagine living her life any other way. "When I started acting, it was just something I thought was fun and neat. I've never really thought about any other roads to take."

The way her career is going, she won't have to.

An Only Child, Jodie Sweetin Finds a Full House

A long line of children snakes down the street. The kids are cheering, clapping, chanting, "We want Jodie!"

It's April 11, 1992, the start of Illinois' first Kids Count Expo. The children are waiting to meet, photograph, and shake hands with a TV star. That star, Jodie Sweetin, is only ten years old. Still, one young fan screams when Jodie gives her a signed photo. Another young fan starts crying.

As Stephanie on *Full House*, Jodie has found her way into the hearts of kids—and grown-ups—all over the country. But she insists, "My life is just like a normal kid's, in a way. I have friends and they all treat me like a regular kid." And for that, says Jodie, she's extremely grateful.

A Fast Start

Jodie Sweetin was born on January 19, 1982, in Los Angeles. She started acting when she was only four years old. Early on, Jodie was recognized as an especially talented youngster. Her mother's friends encouraged her to enroll Jodie in acting classes and to let her go out on auditions.

When Mrs. Sweetin agreed, Jodie's sunny personality quickly did the rest, earning the young blonde four national commercials. Then she made a cameo appearance on the TV show *Valerie*, showing off her winning smile and natural acting style. The producers of *Valerie* were the talented and successful team of Thomas Miller and Robert Boyett. As it happened, Miller and Boyett were also in the process of developing a new sitcom, *Full House*. Jodie's performance on *Valerie* wowed the two producers. They offered her the role of Stephanie without so much as an audition!

A Full Schedule

As a lead on a sitcom, Jodie now has a busy working schedule. Jodie says she loves it. But she's happy whenever summer comes around, since actors on a sitcom get their summers off.

"I enjoy going to work," says Jodie, "but it's nice to have a good long break and see my friends."

During the year when *Full House* is taping, Jodie doesn't get to go to school that often, and she has to work extra hard to keep up with her classmates.

"When I'm on the set, I'm tutored for school," Jodie explains. "I do the same exact work as my class. My teacher gave me an extra set of books, and every week she sends the worksheets and the plans for what the class is doing. I do the work with my tutor on workdays (Monday through Thursday) and on Fridays I go to my regular school. Actually," says Jodie, "it's easier than going to school because we can work one on one and

Jodie on the set.

the tutor can help us more. Still," she adds with a hint of regret, "I really love school."

Pretend Sisters

Jodie says Stephanie is "a really great character to play, because she's real perky and very nice." And as

Jodie grows up in real life and on the show, she's delighted to be dealing with some of the more mature plot problems that used to be reserved for D.J., Stephanie's older sister.

D. J., Michelle, and Stephanie.

In real life, Jodie's an only child. Being on the show "sort of helps me realize what it would be like to have sisters," says Jodie. "It's fun to imagine."

Jodie lives with her parents, her dog Lacey, and her two fish, Spot and Goldie, in Cypress, California. "I have a lot of hobbies," says Jodie. "Some of them are rollerblading, riding bikes, dancing, reading."

What does she want to be when she grows up? It's

a little early to decide, of course, but Jodie's sure of one thing. She wants to go to college. At the moment, some of the careers that appeal to her are being a teacher, a pediatrician, or an astronaut.

Among her co-workers and friends, Jodi is known for being remarkably pleasant and well-adjusted. Quite a feat for a ten-year-old who's showered with fan mail every week.

Jodie's mom, Janice Sweetin, says she and her husband have always been concerned that Jodie's acting career might deprive of her of growing-up time. "We try to give her as much of a normal life as possible. Obviously, it can't be totally normal when she's approached for autographs. From the beginning, though, we've taught her that this begins and it ends. You're a regular person, and when this show ends, you will still be that person, and you'll have to go on from there. Enjoy it now and have fun, but know that it's just a fun experience that will be over."

Thanks to her parents, Jodie maintains a healthy down-to-earth attitude. And that may explain some of her popularity among young TV viewers. Jodie sums up the acting experience this way: "It's hard work, but it pays off because it makes people happy."

On June 13, 1986, in Los Angeles, twin girls were born—Mary Kate and Ashley Olsen. Everyone agreed these two babies were extremely cute. But could anyone have known these two tiny sisters would soon become big TV stars?

Because of child labor laws, *Full House* was looking for twins to share the single role of Danny Tanner's youngest daughter, Michelle (who was nine months old in the show's first episode). Infants are allowed only 20 minutes on camera each day. The producers needed look-alike babies who could alternate on camera. So *Full House* held baby auditions, with baby after baby crawling around the producers' office!

Encouraged by friends, Mrs. Olsen took her nine-month-old daughters to a children's agent. Now it was Mary Kate and Ashley's turn to crawl around the producers'

Introducing Michelle

Mary Kate Olsen.

floor. And on their very first "audition" the Olsen girls landed a starring role on the show.

"We wanted this baby to grow up like a normal baby," says Bob Boyett, one of *Full House*'s three executive producers. "If the baby cried in the middle of the scene, we had to learn how to live with that. No one had ever done that before. The actors on the show embraced the idea, and a bond was created between that little baby and those people."

...and Michelle!!!

How Do You Tell Them Apart?

The twins are now six, and, in real life, live in a full house of their own, with their parents Jamie and Dave, their brother Trent, eight, and their younger sister Elizabeth, three. When away from the *Full House* set, "Ash" and "MK" both love playing outdoors with their family and friends, drawing in their

Ashley Olsen.

coloring books, and riding their pink bicycles.

Friends say it's not hard to tell them apart. As identical as they appear on the show, the Olsens are actually fraternal, not identical twins. (Fraternal twins don't look exactly alike.) Ashley is the oldest (by two minutes) and is right-handed. Mary Kate favors her left. But according to their co-stars, even bigger differences have developed over the years. These differences have come into play in deciding which scenes should be played by which girl. Though both share a good sense of humor, Ashley tends to be more outgoing than Mary Kate. The *Full House* producers take advantage of this difference by often using Ashley in scenes that call for Michelle to be spunky or excited. Mary Kate is often used in those scenes that feature a more sensitive, quiet Michelle.

Does sharing one role lead to jealousy? Not according to their on-set tutor, who says the little girls rarely fight. In fact, like most twins, the young Olsens are thoroughly devoted to each other. Often when a question is asked, they reply together. When they were younger, the twins used to drop off to sleep with their heads, arms, and legs in identical positions!

Growing Up on TV

Over the first five seasons, Michelle has been growing up on the show, just as the Olsen twins have been growing up off-screen. Television audiences have witnessed such heartwarming milestones as the twins learning to walk and talk, mastering the two-wheel bicycle, and making the transition from crib to "big-girl" bed.

Audiences have responded to such scenes in a big way. TV networks are always taking polls and testing how much the audience likes the different stars. In what are known as TVQ ratings, these polls rank all the actors from best-liked to least-liked. In TVQ popularity for girls on TV, Mary Kate and Ashley are often rated number one!

"You got it, dude!"

"You talking to me?"

"Whoa baby!"

Those are a few of the phrases Michelle has made famous on *Full House*. She's so famous, in fact, that in 1991 toy manufacturers came out with a Michelle doll! When you hug her, Michelle says one of her well-known lines.

Not only that, the two girls recently completed filming a TV movie all their own. The director is Jeff Franklin, *Full House*'s creator, so the twins should feel right at home!

The film is called *To Grandmother's House We Go*. In it, the Olsens play twin daughters who head off to visit their grandmother. Along the way, they meet up with evil villains.

Will they make it?

"You got it, dude!"

And does the future look bright for these twin actresses?

"Whoa baby!" Does it ever!

Meet *Full House* Heartthrob John Stamos

The car is a 1969 baby-blue Mustang convertible. But it's hard to see at the moment, because it's surrounded by a swarm of excited girls.

The girls are screaming and snapping pictures. They're struggling for a close-up glimpse of the car's driver, a stunningly handsome young man with dark, magnetic eyes and jet-black hair—John Stamos.

Ever since he started acting, John's been a regular on the cover of every teen magazine. And when this teen idol plays drums with the Beach Boys, the girls scream for him. Still, John insists there are only four women for him—Becky, D.J.,

Becky and Jesse.

Steph, and Michelle, his TV wife and nieces on *Full House*!

John Stamos is going into his sixth season as Uncle Jesse Katsopolis, Danny Tanner's musician brother-in-law. Fans of the show have become used to seeing their heartthrob dangling helplessly above the stage as his attempted rock concert turns to disaster, or accidentally locking himself and pal Joey into his new recording studio, or sticking his face smack into a bowl of cereal! Week after week, John's comic timing has shown fans he's much more than just a handsome face. He's an excellent comedian as well.

Executive Producer Tom Miller remembers worrying whether they'd find someone who could really play Jesse to the max. Miller says great-looking men who can do comedy are rare. He adds, "We were looking for someone who was not afraid to take comedic chances and wouldn't mind committing to moments of inspired nuttiness, because you can't be at all concerned about how you look."

Though he is routinely voted one of the country's handsomest men and was on *People* magazine's short list of the world's most beautiful people, John Stamos has shown he's not worried about his image.

"I love the process of acting," says John. "I love to work at it and make something good. I love to rehearse a scene all week and then on Friday night just nail it and say, 'I did my best.'"

Joey and Becky laughing at Jesse.

A Stamos is Born!

On August 19, 1963, John was born to Bill and Loretta Stamos of Orange County, California. (His family name was originally Stamotopoulos. His grandfather shortened it to Stamos when he left Greece and came to America.) John's father, Bill, runs several fast-food restaurants. Bill and Loretta's son was a born performer. According to Loretta, John got interested in acting "somewhere between the delivery room and the nursery!"

"I was always showing off, doing stupid stuff for laughs, and getting in trouble," remembers John.

As a little boy, he loved to sing and dance for his parents and his younger sisters, Janine and Alaina. Then, when he was nine, he started playing drums.

Soon he was banging and knocking and bopping up enough of a storm to shake up the whole house. Drumming was "a real release," says John. By high school, he had formed his own band, called Destiny.

At the time, John wasn't sure which he preferred— acting or music. For the most part he was, in his own words, "a band nerd."

"I didn't like high school," confesses John. "Instead of going to a lot of high school dances, I was playing with my band. So a lot of people didn't like me for that!"

A School Trip Changes John's Destiny

In junior high, John's drama class took a trip to see the backstage workings of a live TV show, *Happy Days* (produced by none other than Tom Miller and Bob Boyett). John and the producers were destined to cross paths again soon—but not yet.

Watching *Happy Days*, John began to realize just how much he wanted to act. So after high school he went to interview with a theatrical agent. John's sparkling eyes and winning smile usually make a good first impression. The agent quickly sent him on an audition for ABC's soap opera, *General Hospital.* It was John's first audition ever, and he got the part!

The role was supposed to last only five days. But that was before thousands of young girls across the country got a look at John. Letters flooded ABC's offices, demanding to see more of John's character in the future.

The show's producers were only too happy to oblige, and John found himself with a regular starring role.

"Aren't You the Guy. . .?"

Despite John's sudden fame, his father still didn't trust acting as a career, and kept John working as a part-time cook at one of his restaurants.

"I told my dad the show was number one, but he said he couldn't replace me," recalls John, laughing at the memory. "So for a month and a half I worked on Sundays, flipping burgers, taking orders, and studying my script. People would come in and say, 'Aren't you the guy...?'"

John's soap acting brought him an Emmy nomination and a Soapy Award from *Soap Opera Digest* magazine. Deciding it was time for even bigger challenges, John left *General Hospital*. He landed a starring role in a CBS series about a rock group. It was called *Dreams*. But then came his first hard knock. The series quickly failed.

"It hit me hard," says Stamos. "On *General Hospital* I kind of fit in there. It just happened. Things were handed to me. Then it didn't work. It was not as easy as I thought it would be. After *Dreams*, I went to New York for a few months, taking acting classes and auditioning for plays."

Though it was disappointing, John credits that period as an important time for learning about himself,

and learning his craft. His next sitcom attempt (*You Again?*, NBC) paired him with Jack Klugman of *Odd Couple* fame. On the show, Klugman and Stamos played a father and son who hadn't seen each other for seven years. Though this show also flopped, John felt he learned a great deal from veteran star Klugman.

"When he first came on the show, he had the dynamics, but he didn't have a long concentration span," Klugman remembers. "I told him to do what James Cagney (an actor from the 1940s) did: look the other actor in the eye and tell him the truth."

John took the advice to heart, and he kept working and studying. By 1987, when he started taping *Full House*, John found himself in the role of show-biz veteran, with a lot more acting experience than either of his standup-comic co-stars, Bob Saget and Dave Coulier. Indeed, the two comedians looked to John for acting advice and tips on TV performing.

Hunk or Dork?

After the first season, John shortened his shoulder-length hair. He did this because his character was pursuing a career in advertising and needed a more conservative look. Not only that, John thought it was time to shed his teen image and begin to move on.

Luckily, the new short haircut didn't seem to cut into John's appeal. In fact, John has since been voted one of the world's 10 most eligible bachelors (*Us* magazine) and one of the world's 50 most beautiful people (*People* magazine). Still, John refuses to think of himself that way.

"I think you always see yourself the way you are as a kid," he explains. "I was kind of dorky."

Be that as it may, John has never been at a loss for dates. Eight years ago, he even had a few dates with his *Full House* character's future wife, Lori Loughlin. His most gossiped-about romance came in 1990. He was involved with pop star Paula Abdul.

Says Abdul of the relationship, "John will always be someone I can count on. He's the funniest guy I've ever been around. And also," she jokes affectionately, "an incredible geek."

Abdul and Stamos have remained very close friends, talking to each other on the phone almost every day. "The breakup was my fault," John says. "I really couldn't handle her fame and everything that surrounds it."

Choosing Marriage

Today, John says longingly that his greatest fantasy is to "find someone I'm really in love with and start a family and be happy."

While he waits for the right woman to come along, though, he's found he can control his make-believe destiny on *Full House*. At one point the producers asked him, "Should you get married, or do you want to date a new girl every episode?" For John, the choice was easy. Jesse and Rebecca were soon married.

The next season, another off-screen wish of John's came true, when the producers gave Jesse and Rebecca twin sons. Off-screen, John's love of children has him working for the Starlight Foundation, taking kids who are very sick on trips to nearby Disneyland.

Bang the Drums Loudly

What does John do during each year's break, when *Full House* isn't filming? He likes to spend his time in two very different ways. He rides his motorcycle on long solitary trips. And he tours with the Beach Boys as a drummer!

"Playing with the Beach Boys is always a thrill," says the multitalented Stamos, "like living out my childhood dream. They were the first group I ever saw in concert."

At the same time, John has also begun making feature films. He stunned audiences with his chilling portrayal of a murderer in ABC's true story *Captive*.

"Eventually," says the happy actor, "I want to do only features." And someday after that, "I want to leave Los Angeles and raise a family somewhere else!"

In the meantime though, John Stamos—and his fans—are loving every minute of his star-studded career.

Dave Coulier—
Class Clown Makes Good

When you think of Joey Gladstone on *Full House* you probably think of a lovable, goofy, standup comic who's had to struggle in his comedy career.

Now meet the real Joey Gladstone—Dave Coulier, a lovable, goofy, standup comic who's had to struggle in his comedy career!

There are, of course, some differences. The character Joey is *still* struggling. But in real life, *Full House* has launched the blond-haired Coulier into stardom. In fact, Dave's full schedule now includes not just one hit show, but two. He has taken on the job of co-host on ABC's *America's Funniest People*.

That show is a spin-off of *America's Funniest Home Videos*, hosted by none other than Dave's *Full House* co-star, Bob Saget. Did Saget help his old pal Coulier land the job? Dave says no. "The producers saw me on *Arsenio Hall*," says Coulier with a happy shrug, "and they said, 'This is our guy.'" (Coulier does admit, however, that he and Saget have begun teasing their fellow star, John Stamos. They want to know when *he* is going to get a job hosting *America's Funniest Dishwashers*.)

Dave on Skates? No Joke!

Dave Coulier was born on September 21, 1959, in Detroit, Michigan, and was raised in the nearby suburb of St. Claire Shores. Comedy wasn't Dave's first goal in life— the hockey net was. As a teenager, he was a star of his high school hockey team. He was talented enough to dream of a pro hockey career. An avid athlete, the broadly built young man also excelled in water skiing and swimming.

But at the same time, Coulier was discovering he had strange voices inside himself! And these voices and impersonations tended to pop out at odd moments, to the delight and amuse- ment of his

Joey and Michelle in hockey gear.

teammates and friends. While Dave was still a teen, his comic routines brought him his first comedy job—performing (and writing) commercial voice-overs at a local radio station.

With his great love of both sports and comedy, Coulier's career was at a crossroads. As it turned out, the turning point came at Christmas, when Dave was just 17. During a hockey game, he was bringing the puck out from behind his own net when suddenly, out of nowhere, an opposing player slammed into him.

"I woke up in the hospital," remembers Coulier, "and they were stitching my face up. I remember seeing a needle and thread being pulled from my face. My bones were broken. There was quite a bit of blood. My dad said, 'You're pretty banged up.'"

This story is a rare thing for Coulier—it's not funny. The accident left Dave with a permanent scar. It also helped him make up his mind. Right then and there, Dave decided that making silly noises, doing nutty voices, and making people laugh would be a better—and safer—way to make a living!

Mr. Couch Potato

Dave started doing standup in local Detroit clubs. At 19, he took the plunge and moved to Los Angeles. There he became an overnight success and lived happily ever after . . . *No!*!

Dave remembers an eight-month stretch when he

Joey teaching Michelle how to do Bullwinkle.

was too broke to afford transportation around Los Angeles. It had been eight months since his last standup job. That Thanksgiving was a lonely one. He couldn't afford to fly home to Michigan to be with his family. Dave's life was following his character's, Joey Gladstone, but without the laughs.

On the other hand, Dave had the support of his best friend to help him through the rough times. Just as in the show, his best friend was Bob Saget.

"We've always been like brothers—I say he's the sister I never had," says Saget. "I've even had dinner at his dad's house in Detroit and slept in his old room. Once, Dave stayed on my couch for three weeks. He'd pretend he was my bizarre nephew, Busby, and do funny voices."

A Foot in the Door

Finally, Dave got his first big break. It wasn't exactly glamorous. He landed the job of doorman at the famed Los Angeles comedy club, the Comedy Store. He soon worked his way onto the stage and began collecting the gags and funny characters that are his trademarks. This led to appearances on *Showtime's Laff-a-Thon,* and *HBO's Detroit Comedy Jam.*

Thanks to the funny voices that had made Dave a class clown, the young comedian started getting work on Saturday morning cartoons. He twisted his vocal chords around such character voices as Scooby Doo and Mork in the cartoon version of *Mork and Mindy.* If you tune in to *Muppet Babies* some time, see if you can recognize Dave's voice as Animal and Bunsen Honeydew. His colorful vocal performances won him an Emmy!

By this time, Dave was getting to be well known in the business. Now he not only had money to travel, he was on the road 42 weeks out of the year, performing at comedy clubs across the nation. Then, in 1987, he landed his starring role on *Full House* and left standup behind, without regrets.

"Standup is a grind, man," comments Dave. "It's the hardest thing I've done! You never know when you're going to die one night in front of 300 people. On a sitcom, you can always say, 'The writers didn't come up with the right joke there!'"

Does he mind competing for laughs with his old friend and fellow standup comic co-star, Bob Saget? "We're best friends," Coulier says firmly. "There's no jealousy on our show."

Saget agrees. "He makes me laugh more than anyone else. He's the kind of guy who sticks his head out the car window and yells something and it's funny and you don't mind."

Is Dad Funny?

Dave's son Luc is now two years old. "We watch *Sesame Street* in the morning. We sing the songs and we play. Sometimes I think Luc's looking at me thinking, 'Boy, you must have had low grades.'"

Of course, that's not what most TV fans think when they watch Dave's antics. Most viewers are thinking there will always be room on TV's *Full House* for this warm and funny talent.

Cast with executive producer and creator Jeff Franklin and the 100th episode cake.

Lori Loughlin Takes a Trip Down the Yellow Brick Road

By the time she was four or five years old, Lori Loughlin knew she wanted to be an actress. Lori explains, "I had seen the *Wizard of Oz*, and I wanted to go down the yellow brick road!"

Today the dark-haired and beautiful Loughlin is 27 and it seems she has found her way down that yellow brick road. Starring on *Full House* as the level-headed Rebecca Donaldson-Katsopolis, Lori has endeared herself to millions of TV fans.

A Model Friend

Lori was born on Long Island, New York. She was 11 years old when a friend asked her if she wanted to go

together to a modeling-agency interview. Lori tagged along and found herself quickly signed to the children's division of the prestigious Ford Modeling Agency. She began working immediately, shooting catalog ads for J.C. Penney, Macy's, and Maybelline.

By 16, Lori was pursuing acting. She soon landed the role of Jody Travis on the daytime drama, *The Edge of Night*.

"I played Jody for three years," says Lori, "and the only way to explain her is to say she was the Nancy Drew of daytime."

It was a character Lori played easily and extremely well. But at the same time, Lori's acting success was leaving her little time for her own adolescence—or high school.

"People who knew me in high school thought I was stuck up. I wasn't there much, and when I was, I was uncomfortable. When people first meet me, they think I'm standoffish," says Lori. "Because I'm shy."

Shy or not, Lori's acting career was soon in high gear. When she left the soap, she was immediately cast in her first starring role opposite Eric Stoltz and James Spader in a horror-thriller for Columbia Pictures called *The New Kids*.

Other movie roles followed (*Secret Admirer*, and TV movies *North Beach and Rawhide* and *Brotherhood of Justice* opposite Keanu Reeves and Kiefer Sutherland), but it was her place in Miller and Boyett's *Full House* that would make Lori Loughlin a household name.

A Happy Family

"I know that most of the actors in a sitcom say they are one happy family," says Lori, "but I have to add my voice to the many and say it once again. We get along very well."

Lori and her investment-banker husband Michael moved from New York to Los Angeles when she landed the TV role. "I was brought on to supply a romantic angle for John Stamos's Jesse," explains Lori. "And the chemistry really worked because the letters started coming in. At one point, the producers were thinking of having me paired off with Saget's Danny, but after the reaction to Jesse and Rebecca, they dropped that idea."

Lori doesn't mind leaving her character's romantic fate in the hands of the producers and writers. But she does admit that she finds Rebecca's steady calmness a little frustrating. "She never has any conflicts and is always the voice of reason," says Lori. "Just once I'd like to see her have some problems."

If Lori had to describe her own personality she would say, "Happy, calm"—so far, much like Rebecca Donaldson—"and wildly neurotic." But in a *Full House* crowded with wacky comics, needy children, babies, friends, and pets, Lori may have to stick to her role of being solid and dependable.

Lori works hard to avoid being typecast outside the show. When she got a chance to play a revenge-hungry woman in *A Stranger in the Mirror*, an ABC-TV movie, Lori jumped at the part. She happily describes her character in that film as "conniving!"

Lori's personal hero is Sally Field, "because she turned her career around. People thought of her as only the Flying Nun and Gidget. She had to develop her talent and then show people in the industry and herself and the public what she could do. That's a long, hard road."

It may be a hard road. But the talented Lori Loughlin has already shown that when she sets a goal, she gets there. We can count on seeing many other sides of Lori Loughlin in her future movie career!

Congratulations, Mr. and Mrs. Katsopolis! It's...Two Boys!

Show business is tough. On a sitcom, even the babies have to audition! When the producers of *Full House* were looking for a cute pair of boys to play the role of Jesse and Becky's twin newborns, they auditioned pair after pair of babies. They finally settled on four-month-old Blake and Dylan Tuomy-Wilhoit.

On the show the Tuomy-Wilhoits play Nicholas and Alexander. (The writers picked the name Nicholas in honor of the character Jesse's TV dad Nick, and chose both names because they were typically Greek.)

Why was it so hard to find the right actors for the roles of Nicholas and Alexander? The producers really were hoping to find star-quality triplets, or even quadruplets!

After their experience with the Olsen twins, the producers knew firsthand about filming babies. They knew they would need all the extra camera time they could get to obey the child labor laws about baby actors.

"We weren't able to find triplets or quadruplets who could play Jesse and Becky's twins," explains executive producer and creator Jeff Franklin, "so we're using twins to play twins, which means very limited camera time. And when a twin gets cranky, you don't have that backup baby available to give you a second shot at the scene!"

New Kids on the Block

Has the arrival of the babies changed life backstage for the *Full House* family? Do twins Mary Kate and Ashley feel jealous of the new arrivals for taking over their position as the youngest on the show? The answer, apparently, is that they're no more jealous than the character they play. Michelle got over her anxiety about the twins taking her place in the show's 100th episode —which was the twins' very first.

Adria Later, the schoolteacher who tutors the Olsens on the set, says, "Now they're not the babies anymore. That means they're the Big Girls, and they love it. They feel grown up and they're going to take care of the Tuomy-Wilhoits."

"Oh, the Olsens are fine," adds Jeff Franklin. "It's interesting to see how kids enjoy taking care of other kids. They've been very understanding and patient with the new babies and like to play with them."

John Stamos likes playing with the babies as well. And he's found that every time he tells the twin babies that they look like Fred Mertz (a bald character on the famous *I Love Lucy* TV show), the infants both chuckle.

My, What a Cute Belly Pad!

Lori Loughlin, who plays the babies' mom, may be closest to the newcomers. After all, she pretended to be pregnant with the twins for months. While the search was on for baby actors, Lori had to wear padding on the show, to make it look like she was really pregnant. She found that even carrying around fake babies can get to be a burden.

"I had been wearing the padding for some time, and it got to the point where I just wanted to have those babies," Loughlin laughs. "I put the pad on and started doing that walk and I found that I just had to go lie down. Everybody came up and put their hands on my stomach. It was like a magnet."

Why did the show's writers decide to give Jesse and Rebecca children so soon? After all, the characters had been married for only one season. Lori Loughlin explains, "I think the reason they rushed Jesse and Rebecca into having children was because the show is based so much around kids and families that they really wanted to get more babies on the show."

"Having kids seemed like the next natural step," agrees producer Jeff Franklin. "We had already done something no one had done before in having Michelle grow up right in front of America. And we said, 'How do we top that?' We decided that having Jesse and Rebecca have twins made it new and interesting."

Over the past five seasons, millions of television viewers have delighted in watching Michelle change and grow. What the producers are hoping is that over

the next few seasons, Nicholas and Alexander will
provide that same delight—times two!

Olsen twins with the new Nicky and Alex.

Birth of a Show

It's hard to imagine now, but there once was a time when *Full House* didn't exist. It was only a gleam in the eye of a talented writer-director-producer named Jeff Franklin.

A former schoolteacher and an experienced sitcom writer, Jeff started with the idea of an alternative family. He envisioned a household where men had to raise children without a woman's help—something not on TV at the time.

He took the idea to two top producers he had worked with in the past, Tom Miller and Bob Boyett.

TV Masterminds

Talk about a successful team. Miller, 46, is a Milwaukee native and former assistant film director. Boyett, also 46, is from Atlanta and began his career as a playwright. He ended up working at ABC at the same time Miller was producing *Happy Days*. The two formed a team. Together Miller and Boyett have brought a seemingly endless string of blockbuster hits to TV, shows like *Laverne & Shirley, Mork & Mindy, Bosom Buddies,* and *Family Matters*.

Franklin, Miller, and Boyett added *Full House* to their list. The Friday night comedy proved so popular that when ABC first moved the show to a Tuesday night slot, fans young and old were outraged at the change in their viewing routine.

Boyett says he has a basic formula for success in a comedy show: "What keeps a sitcom going is your ability to present characters people want to follow."

Keeping the growth of their characters firmly in mind, the producers meet regularly with their large staff of writers. Once the producers and writers have all agreed on a story idea, the writers prepare a beat sheet. The beat sheet describes each scene of the proposed show in a few sentences. Then one writer is assigned to write a ten-page outline.

The producers go over the outline, making sure their characters are all acting like themselves. The writer turns the outline into a first draft. The staff rewrites that script. And after all this hard work, the writing process has still just begun!

The Table Reading

Now the cast gathers for what's called a table reading. The actors all sit around a big table so the producers and writers can hear the new script out loud.

Next step? More work for the writers, as they fix up the jokes that didn't get big laughs at the table reading. They also tighten the spots where the story lagged.

Meanwhile, a production meeting is held to talk about all the different elements of the show, such as special sets that must be designed, or costumes that need to be bought or made.

The cast rehearses for four days. "On *Full House*, we have dogs, four-year-old twins, an eight-year-old girl, a 13-year-old girl, and 2 standup comics who have other shows," director Joel Zwick once told reporters. "Directing this show is more like real life than a television show. It's an organizational feat to do *Full House*."

The writers are on hand during all the craziness of rehearsals, making last-minute changes. Finally, in the middle of the week, the cast gets to take home the script and memorize their lines.

For the last rehearsal, the cast rehearses in front of the cameras, so that the camera operators can see what they'll be shooting and the director can experiment with different camera angles. And then—at long last—it's showtime. . . .

The Final Cut

Full House is performed before a live audience. You can hear their roars of laughter in the background as you watch each Tuesday night. That audience sees a lot you don't see, however. Since the show is filmed live, the studio audience has the fun of seeing the actors mess up, make mistakes, and redo scenes.

After shooting, the show is still not done. Now the film editor has three days to do the first cut. Then the director asks for changes. The producers watch the episode and make their final cuts. It is the producers' job to cut the show down to its final length.

To make room for commercials, a half-hour TV sitcom can last only between 22 and 23 minutes.

Except for music, sound effects, and opening titles and credits, the show is finally done. The tape is delivered to ABC.

The next time you tune in to *Full House,* think about this. The half hour of entertainment you're about to watch actually took about six weeks and the work of many people to create. Now it's ready for you to enjoy!

Jeff Franklin talking to John Stamos.

Your *Full House* Checklist

Producers of sitcoms keep a guide to every past episode of the show. On a hit comedy such as *Full House,* that's a long list. Now heading into its sixth season (with more than 20 shows a season), *Full House* has quickly developed a long and complex history, just like a real-life family.

That's why a list of shows comes in so handy. Let's say the show's writers want Stephanie to refer back to her ballet debut in season one, episode six. Checking the guide will tell them that Steph debuted as a flying swan.

The guide's great for fans as well. For one thing, you can check out just how many shows you've seen. Then watch for repeats of your missing shows as you try to fill in all your gaps.

SEASON ONE, 1987-88

☐ **1. Our Very First Show** — Widowed father Danny Tanner enlists the aid of his brother-in-law, Jesse, and his best friend, Joey, to help him raise his children.

☐ **2. Our Very First Night** —The girls are rockin' when Uncle Jesse is left in charge for the night.

☐ **3. The First Day of School** — Stephanie's reluctant to attend her first day of school.

☐ **4. The Return of Grandma** — An untimely visit from the guys' mothers turns the house upside down.

☐ **5. Sea Cruise** — Danny's all-male fishing trip turns into a love-boat cruise.

☐ **6. Daddy's Home** — Danny has to fly off to work minutes before Stephanie makes her ballet debut as a flying swan.

☐ **7. Knock Yourself Out** — Danny's tryout for a career as a boxing announcer isn't exactly a knockout.

☐ **8. Jesse's Girl** —Jesse's new dream girl turns into a nightmare when she dumps him for Joey.

☐ **9. Our Very First Promo** — The Tanner family is thrilled when they are chosen to appear in a local promo at Danny's TV station.

☐ **10. The Miracle of Thanksgiving**— It's a turkey of a day when everyone teams up to prepare the Thanksgiving feast.

☐ **11. Joey's Place** — Joey feels blue when he starts getting ready for a two-week comedy tour. The family starts acting like he's gone even before he leaves.

☐ **12. The Big Three-O** — Danny crashes his own surprise 30th birthday party, only to discover that Jesse has dunked his prize car in the bay.

☐ **13. Sister Love** — Stephanie is chosen for the part in a TV commercial for which D.J. was auditioning.

☐ **14. Half a Love Story** — Jesse uses baby Michelle to get a date with one of Danny's co-workers.

☐ **15. A Pox in Our House** — Danny's itching to play ball with the Harlem Globetrotters, but his family comes down with chicken pox.

☐ **16. But Seriously Folks** — Joey's convinced that his comic debut in front of a talent scout is jinxed.

☐ **17. Danny's Very First Date**— Danny develops a crush on the hive mother of Stephanie's Honey Bees.

☐ **18. D.J. Tanner's Day Off** — D.J. skips school and sneaks down to the mall to get a celebrity's autograph.

☐ **19. Just One of the Guys** — D.J. feels left out when her cousin visits and spends most of his time roughhousing with Danny.

☐ **20. The Seven-Month Itch, Part I** — Frustrated at his lack of privacy, Jesse heads for the hills.

☐ **20. The Seven-Month Itch, Part II** —The girls scheme to bring Uncle Jesse back home.

☐ **21. Mad Money** — Jesse secretly plans a nightclub Elvis tribute, while Joey attempts to pay back Danny the money he lent him 11 years ago.

SEASON TWO, 1988-89

☐ **22. Cutting It Close** — After an accident, Stephanie is convinced she's a jinx.

☐ **23. Tanner *vs.* Gibbler** — Danny becomes a talk show host on *Wake Up San Francisco.*

☐ **24. It's Not My Job** —Jesse tells his father he's leaving the family bug-killing business. Stephanie gets her first cavity.

☐ **25. Jingle Bell** —Jesse takes Joey on as a partner. Danny's having trouble getting Michelle potty-trained.

☐ **26. D.J.'s First Horse** — D.J. and Kimmy buy a horse. Jesse strikes out in his attempts to date Rebecca.

☐ **27. Joey Gets Tough** —While Jesse's band makes a guest appearance on Danny's show, Joey gets his turn at baby-sitting.

☐ **28. Beach Boy Bingo** — D.J. wins a "Dream Night with the Beach Boys" radio contest.

☐ **29. Middle Age Crazy** — Middle child Stephanie struggles for attention.

☐ **30. Our Very First Christmas Show** —Bad weather forces the family to spend Christmas in the airport. Jesse gets a kiss from Rebecca.

☐ **31. Triple Date** — Danny invites his date over only to find that the woman is still carrying a torch for Jesse.

☐ **32. A Little Romance** — The guys participate in a charity bachelor auction. D.J.'s boyfriend breaks her heart.

☐ **33. Fogged In** —Jesse's quarreling parents get fogged in at the Tanner house, where Jesse is fighting with D.J.

☐**34. Working Mothers** —Joey and Jesse start a full-time job at an ad agency, only to discover they miss being Mr. Moms.

☐ **35. Little Shop of Sweaters** — D.J. and Stephanie inadvertently shoplift a sweater.

☐ **36. Pal Joey** — Danny feels left out when Joey spends more time with Jesse. Stephanie gets mad at D.J. for "stealing" her crush.

☐ **37. Baby Love**—Michelle is distraught when Rebecca's two-year-old nephew, her new friend, has to leave.

☐ **38. El Problema Grande de D.J.**—To her annoyance, D.J.'s D grade in Spanish ends up leading to a date for Danny.

☐ **39. Goodbye Mr. Bear** — During spring cleaning, Joey accidentally gives Stephanie's Mr. Bear to the Salvation Army.

☐ **40. Blast from the Past**— Joey rekindles an old romance. Amateur magician Kimmy handcuffs D.J. and Stephanie together.

☐ **41. I'm There for You Babe** — The Tanner family fills in when Jesse forgets to book his band for a gig.

☐ **42. Luck Be a Lady, Part I** — The Tanners go on location with *Wake Up San Francisco* to Lake Tahoe. Jesse proposes to Rebecca.

☐ **42. Luck Be a Lady, Part II** — Becky accepts Jesse's marriage proposal, and the couple sneaks off to a chapel, only to be joined by the entire Tanner family.

SEASON THREE, 1989-90

☐ **43. Tanner's Island** — Danny takes the family on a surprise trip to Hawaii and gets them lost on the island of Pua.

☐ **44. Back To School Blues** — D.J. and Kimmy suffer through their first day of junior high.

☐ **45. Breaking Up Is Hard to Do (in 22 Minutes)** — Jesse and Rebecca break up, and D.J. and Stephanie try to get them back together.

☐ **46. Nerd for a Day** — Stephanie learns the hard way that being teased feels terrible.

☐ **47. Granny Tanny** — When Danny's mother visits, the family plays helpless, so she'll feel needed.

☐ **48. Star Search** —Joey tries to recharge his comedy career by going on *Star Search*.

☐ **49. And They Call It Puppy Love** —The Tanner family takes in a stray dog and gets more than they bargained for: puppies.

☐ **50. Divorce Court** — With D.J. and Stephanie at odds, the guys set up a mock court to settle the girls' differences.

☐ **51. Dr. Dare Rides Again** — When an old pal of Jesse's comes into town, Jesse feels like he has to prove he's still a wild, happening dude.

☐ **52. The Greatest Birthday on Earth** — Michelle, Jesse, and Stephanie miss Michelle's third birthday party.

☐ **53. Misadventures in Baby-Sitting** — Wanting to earn money for a phone of her own, D.J. tries baby-sitting.

☐ **54. Joey and Stacey and...Oh Yeah, Jesse** —Jesse and Joey's friendship is tested when a love interest comes into Joey's life.

☐ **55. Aftershocks** — Stephanie is afflicted by post-earthquake trauma.

☐ **56. Thirteen Candles** — D.J. officially has her first kiss.

☐ **57. No More Mr. Dumbguy** – Jesse sets out to prove to Becky that he can be just as smooth as her visiting college professor.

☐ **58. Bye-Bye Birdie** —Michelle lets the class bird out of the cage and thinks none of the kids like her.

☐ **59. Lust in the Dust** — Neat freak Danny finally meets a woman he likes—only to find out she's a slob.

☐ **60. Mr. Egghead** — Joey gets a job hosting the *Mr. Egghead Show* but bombs miserably—and accidentally breaks Stephanie's nose.

☐ **61. Just Say No Way**— Uncle Jesse catches D.J. holding a beer at a school dance.

☐ **62. Those Better Not Be the Days** — The guys decide to teach the girls a lesson in appreciating others by playing a role-reversal game.

☐ **63. Honey, I Broke the House** — Stephanie accidentally crashes Joey's new car into the house.

☐ **64. Our Very First Telethon—** Danny hosts a telethon for the station, and his family bails him out by performing their own talent acts.

☐ **65. Three Men and Another Baby** — Michelle becomes jealous when the neighbor's baby comes for a visit.

☐ **66. Fraternity Reunion** —With their ten-year fraternity reunion coming up, Joey convinces Danny to participate in a silly fraternity prank. It lands them both in jail.

SEASON FOUR, 1990-91

☐ **67. The I.Q. Man** — Jesse and Joey land a big cologne advertising account. The catch is that Jesse has to model in the commercial.

☐ **68. Greek Week** — Jesse's grandparents visit from Greece, bringing with them the stunning Elena, Jesse's childhood friend. Despite Elena's tempting beauty, Jesse and Rebecca get engaged.

☐ **69. Terror in Tanner Town** — Danny's date Cindy brings her terror of a son over to meet the Tanners. The boy causes chaos.

☐ **70. Good News, Bad News** — D.J. and Kimmy's friendship is in jeopardy when they work together on the school paper.

☐ **71. Crimes and Michelle's Demeanor—** Can the guys be firm parents and lay down the rules for cute Michelle?

☐ **72. Slumber Party** — Stephanie doesn't want to go to her Honey Bee slumber party because she'll be the only one without a mom.

☐ **73. Shape Up—** D.J. goes on a crash diet to prepare for Kimmy's pool party.

☐ **74. Viva Las Joey** —Joey gets to open for Wayne Newton in Las Vegas. But just then his Dad shows up for a stormy reunion.

☐ **75. One Last Kiss** —Jesse is afraid to go to his tenth reunion where he'll have to see his old flame Carrie.

☐ **76. A Pinch for a Pinch** — Jesse becomes a parent volunteer at Michelle's school.

☐ **77. Secret Admirer** — A fake love note causes great confusion at the annual Tanner Family Barbecue.

☐ **78. Happy New Year**—Joey has such a great first date on New Year's Eve that he and the woman decide to get married—that same night.

☐ **79. Danny in Charge**—With Jesse and Joey away on a job, Danny tries to be Super Dad and do everything.

☐ **80. Working Girl** —When D.J. gets a job as a photographer's assistant at the mall, her schoolwork suffers.

☐ **81. Stephanie Gets Framed** — Stephanie is upset when she finds out she has to wear glasses. Danny is upset when Jesse picks Joey to be his best man for the wedding.

☐ **82. A Fish Called Martin** — Michelle is upset by the death of her pet goldfish.

☐ **83. Old Brown Eyes** — D.J. organizes a talent night for her school fund-raiser.

☐ **84. The Wedding, Part I**— Jesse disappears on the day of his wedding.

☐ **84. The Wedding, Part II**— Desperately trying to get to his wedding on time, Jesse gets arrested.

☐ **85. Fuller House** — Jesse and Rebecca talk to Danny about turning the attic into an apartment for them.

☐ **86. The Hole in the Wall Gang** — Feuding and fighting, Steph and D.J. manage to poke a hole in Danny's wall.

☐ **87. Stephanie Plays the Field** —Because she has a crush on one of the players, Stephanie decides to try out for Danny's baseball team.

☐ **88. The Graduates** —Stephanie feels left out when the family gets caught up in the excitement of D.J.'s and Michelle's graduations.

☐ **89. Joey Goes Hollywood** — Joey gets a part on a TV pilot with Frankie Avalon and Annette Funicello.

☐ **90. Girls Just Wanna Have Fun** — D.J. and Kimmy secretly plan to invite two boys over to the house where Kimmy's baby-sitting.

☐ **91. Rock the Cradle** —Jesse is the last to learn that Rebecca is pregnant.

SEASON FIVE, 1991-92

☐ **92. Double Trouble** —Jesse and Rebecca get the news she'll be having twins.

☐ **93. Matchmaker Michelle** — Missing her mommy, Michelle tries to fix Danny up with her preschool teacher, Miss Wiltrout.

☐ **94. Take My Sister, Please** — D.J. and Michelle want their own room. Upset, Steph moves into the bathroom.

☐ **95. Where, Oh Where, Has My Little Girl Gone** —D.J. is the victim of a bad rumor at school.

☐ **96. The King and I** — A man who looks just like Elvis appears to Jesse and gives him some important advice on families.

☐ **97. The Legend of Ranger Joe** — Joey thinks he'll be able to take over from kid host Ranger Roy, host of a kid's TV show.

☐ **98. The Volunteer** — D.J. becomes a volunteer with the Adopt-A-Grandparent program.

☐ **99. Gotta Dance** — Stephanie wants to dedicate herself to a life of dance, but finds rehearsals awfully demanding.

☐ **100. Happy Birthday Babies, Part I**—It's Michelle's fifth birthday, but she's anxious about the upcoming birth of Rebecca's twins.

☐ **100. Happy Birthday Babies, Part II** — Rebecca goes into labor. Jesse comes down with appendicitis.

☐ **101. Nicky and/or Alexander**—Jesse and Rebecca bring Nicky and Alexander home from the hospital.

☐ **102. Bachelor of the Month** —Danny has a crush on his temporary co-host, Vicky. Michelle sneaks along on their first date.

☐ **103. Easy Rider**—Joey tries to teach Michelle how to ride a bike.

☐ **104. Sisters in Crime** — D.J. gets in trouble when she takes her sisters with her on a date.

☐ **105. Play It Again, Jess** — When Rebecca goes back to work, Jesse feels bad about not being the breadwinner.

☐ **106. Crushed** — A teen idol is going to be a guest at Stephanie's tenth birthday.

☐ **107. Spellbound** — Stephanie competes in a spelling bee against Davey Chu, better known as the Human Dictionary.

☐ **108. Too Much Monkey Business** — Danny's sister Wendy visits with her pet monkey.

☐ **109. The Devil Made Me Do It** — Two dream figures appear before Michelle, each offering very different advice.

☐ **110. Driving Miss D.J.**— Both Danny and Jesse have a bad time as D.J.'s first driving instructors.

☐ **111. Yours, Mine, and Ours** — Jesse and Becky keep arguing about their different methods of baby-raising.

☐ **112. The Trouble With Danny**— Danny the clean freak gets upset when the rest of the Tanners aren't into spring cleaning.

☐ **113. Five's A Crowd** — Danny and Jesse try to rescue D.J. from a date at a drive-in movie.

☐ **114. Girls Will be Boys** —After feeling left out when playing with the boys, Michelle goes through a tomboy phase.

☐ **115. Captain Video, Part I** — Joey fires Jesse from his new job as Lumberjack Jess on the *Ranger Joe* show. Jesse gets depressed until Fat Fish Records signs him to make a music video.

☐ **115. Captain Video, Part II** — Jesse's music video is turning into a disaster, until the producers agree to let Jesse shoot it his way.

The Official
Full House Trivia Quiz

So you think you're the ultimate *Full House* fan. You've seen almost every show. Then you've got nothing to worry about—you've already done all the cramming for our test of *Full House* stumpers! (Hint: You'll find some of the answers in this book, especially in Your *Full House* Checklist, beginning on page 55.)

When you're done, add up all the points listed for your correct answers. Here's how to judge your score:

700 –1,189 — Amazing! Consider yourself the new president of the *Full House* Trivia Society!

200 – 699 — Okay, so you didn't get every one. But you can still call yourself a true *Full House* expert!

0 – 199 — What's the matter? Been wasting your time watching other shows besides *Full House*?

For the following questions, score 1 point for each correct answer.

1) The name of the talk show hosted by Danny Tanner is _____ .

2) Who's the neat freak—Jesse, Danny, or Joey?

3) Joey lands a job hosting a kids' TV show. What's his name on the show?

4) In real life, one of the actresses has a celebrity actor brother. What's *his* name?

For the following questions, score 5 points for each correct answer:

5) True or false? Danny once tried out as a boxing announcer?

6) Who dunked Danny's prize car in the bay? Jesse, D.J., or Stephanie?

7) Who crashed Joey's car into the house? Jesse, D.J., or Stephanie?

8) The girls' organization Stephanie belongs to is called:

A) The Girl Scouts
B) The Honey Bees
C) The Quilters
D) The Young
   Sisterhood

9) Stephanie once got so upset she moved into what room?

10) What do Scooby Doo, Animal, Mork, and Bunsen Honeydew have in common?

11) During the first season, was Jesse's hair short or long?

Getting a lot harder now. Score 50 points for any correct answer in the following:

12) What business is Jesse's father in?

13) What was the name of Michelle's preschool teacher?

14) Stephanie makes her ballet debut as a
_____ .

15) Jesse briefly worked as Joey's sidekick on his TV show. What was Jesse's name on the show?

16) Stephanie is defeated in a spelling bee by a kid known as the Human Dictionary. What was the child's real name?

17) D.J. and Kimmy buy what kind of animal together?

18) What was the first name of the woman who filled in as co-host on *Wake Up San Francisco* while Rebecca was on maternity leave?

19) Joey misses the chance to open for _____ in Las Vegas.

Okay, here come the mega-blockbuster stumpers. Score 100 points for each correct answer.

20) How old was Michelle in the show's very first episode?

21) Michelle's goldfish was named _____ .

22) Joey bombs when he hosts *The* _____ *Show*.

Last but not least, if you can solve this trick question, score 250 points.

23) On family trips, the Tanners have been to all but one of the following places. Which one?

   A) Pua Island in Hawaii
   B) Lake Tahoe
   C) Colorado

TRIVIA ANSWERS

1. *Wake Up San Francisco*
2. Danny
3. Ranger Joe
4. Kirk Cameron
5. True
6. Jesse
7. Stephanie
8. B
9. The bathroom
10. They're all cartoon characters whose voice is performed by actor Dave Coulier.
11. Long
12. Bug killing
13. Miss Wiltrout
14. flying swan
15. Lumberjack Jess
16. Davey Chu
17. A horse
18. Vicky
19. Wayne Newton
20. Nine months old
21. Martin
22. *Mr. Egghead*
23. It's a trick question because the Tanners were on their way to ski in Colorado in Episode 30. Thanks to a snowstorm, they never got there. Correct answer, C.

Michelle and Jesse.

Want to Write to *Full House*?

Write to your favorite *Full House* character. You can reach them all at this address:

Full House
Studio Fan Mail
1122 S. Robertson Blvd.
Suite 15
Los Angeles, CA 90035